Not Many Love Poems

LINDA CHASE grew up on Long Island, New York and was educated
at Bennington College in Vermont. She later did an MA in creative
writing at Manchester Metropolitan University. In between, she was
a stage costume designer in San Francisco and Edinburgh, and a Tai
Chi teacher, later specialising in Tai Chi for special needs. She lived
in Manchester where she set up the Manchester branch of the Poetry
School and was the founding Director of Poets and Players
(www.poetsandplayers.co.uk), a series of poetry and music perform-
ances. Linda Chase died in April 2011.

Also by Linda Chase from Carcanet Press

The Wedding Spy
Extended Family

LINDA CHASE

Not Many Love Poems

CARCANET

First published in Great Britain in 2011 by
Carcanet Press Limited
Alliance House
Cross Street
Manchester M2 7AQ

www.carcanet.co.uk

A CIP catalogue record for this book is available from the British Library
ISBN 978 1 84777 086 8

The publisher acknowledges financial assistance from Arts Council England

Typeset by XL Publishing Services, Tiverton
Printed and bound in England by SRP Ltd, Exeter

With love, to my grandchildren

Angus, May, Rory and Rowan

Acknowledgements

Thanks are due to the editors of publications in which a number of these poems first appeared. Thanks also to James McGrath for his work on this collection.

'Ray Charles Visits Suite 1, Radiotherapy Department, Christie Hospital, Manchester, England' was Commended in the Poetry Society National Poetry Competition 2007.

Contents

I Many Love Poems

II Kisses and Harps

Kisses

Harps

III   Our Lives

I
Many Love Poems

Our Life

In the 40s we swam
like fish in the water-turtle lake.

In the 50s we went
together on trains along the Hudson.

In the 60s we battled
waves in a storm on Lake George.

In the 70s I threw you
an apple from an upstairs window.

In the 80s I buried
you, just the once

though it feels
like a daily occurrence –

quick strokes,
long glides, sculling.

One Summer Night

We were fourteen and thought that cigarettes
were sophisticated, cool as it gets.
Fireflies were flickering on and off
that night we sat outside and smoked. Your cough,
a punctuation in the heavy heat –
we heard a car, then voices from the street
and finally nothing made a sound except
the intermittent cricket chirps that kept
the night from drifting toward oblivion.
You took my hand, a simple act of union.
Nothing happened next. Our holding hands
was not the start of more elaborate plans.
It was the only thing we wanted then,
connecting worlds of women and of men.

First Thought

> Will you write to me
> as if your life depended on it? Your death too?
> Don't censor, don't delete, don't think things through;
> just let rip straight from your gut, naturally.
> A poor writer might tell little white lies
> to save embarrassment, or else his ass,
> his dignity, his fear, sometimes, his pride.
> But I'm not having it! Open your eyes,
> heart, don't watch what you say, be crude, be crass;
> a true writer is one who never lied.

The Word for It

Nothing separates her from him
or from the warm corduroy of his trousers,
the even warp and weft of his oxford shirt
with its tiny mother-of-pearl buttons keeping
what might fly away, down. Nothing.

He, in those grownup clothes,
joins the softness of her in hers,
her layers of nylon, cotton and tweed,
her lipstick and perfume, still tentative,
as their wrinkling shirts untuck.

Even thoughts of words are stripped.
Here, open mouthed, stunned by where
his fingers have been drawn –
under and inside and inside again
to that place which had been hers, nameless,
that alarmingly secret source
now is blasted open by him
and she has no idea about anything
which could be said in any words she knows
or in any words she used to know.

He wants her to know the word for it
but all she wants to do is hide her shotgun face
in the crook of his arm forever.

Be Home by Midnight

We had started unbuttoning on the sofa
and my hand was nearing your zip
when a sound from upstairs gathered
and rolled down on us, halting us
in the tiny present of only ourselves.
This other presence throbbed with
shallow waves of sorrow, saying
this does not belong to you alone.
Sighs roamed through the house
like heartless jewel thieves in the dark
prising out our private new discoveries.
The Christmas tree lights were still lit
and a scribbled note on the table read,
Please turn lights off when you come in.

Old Flame

He turns my hand in his hand
as if to catch the light,
separating my fingers
to see my rings, one by one.
Questions and answers follow –
country, stones, when, from whom
and then my other hand
because this ritual has been
going on for fifty years
and there are no surprises,
as he counts the parts of me
and the decorations I choose.

But today I wear a bracelet,
he has never seen before,
knowing that it's to his taste,
that it will spark new attention
beyond his routine inspection.
Between the larger stones,
lodge dashes of orange abalone,
keeping spaces in between
irregular chunks of turquoise.
He fingers them around my wrist
and I'm a girl again, fluttering
through her jewellery and her life.

Corsican Summer

Once, driving up a mountain in Corsica,
you talked about storms in Colorado
which turned the trees to ice.
Then wind would make the branches craze
like crystal chandeliers chiming through the night.
You were a kid in your bed, listening.

Tonight, I want you to tell me that story again
although I know every word by heart.

Longing for cold has swamped me
like a huge coat, dragged on the ground.
It's not my coat, my love, and yet
I want each seam – each buttonhole,
the buttons themselves. I want that song
the ice trees sang in the night to a boy.

Fire

She had no map, no snakebite kit,
only the name of the mountain
where he would be looking out
from the top for smoke or smouldering.

It was rattlesnake country, bone dry
and hot and his bed was a narrow bunk
jammed beside the Fire Service radio.
His water had been carried up by mule.

I'm not going to ask you, he whispered
that night as he drew her in close
and the length of their bodies kindled
in bursts before their mouths caught.

Airstream Bubble Trailer

Somehow a double bed
fits across one end
where in day time, a table might be
with two benches facing
and a centre slot for legs.

> This is a tin can miracle
> of convertible space –
> have what you need
> and have it when you need it.
> Airstream stands on its head for you.

But the table is never up
since the bed is needed day and night
and these two can eat and read and write
on their laps, sidestepping necessity
to convert to daytime mode.

> Look! She has enough room
> to dance in just her jeans.
> The radio plays. He watches,
> curled up on the bed with a book.
> He reaches out his hand
> and scoops her breast as it floats
> for a second into his space.

Darwin would be proud of me,
I can adapt, I will survive, she thinks,
whirling toward the dance's end.
Her arms are high, her body spins,
her breasts rise up through centrifugal force.

> She keeps on going faster
> and then before she knows it,
> she's flung herself beside him on the bed.
> 'Read to me,' she says, eyes closed,
> and he begins, 'I saw the best
> minds of my generation…'

The Tao tells me to go on loving you

Still, those long yellow legal pads let
philosophy tuck itself in beside love.
I see your letter every day on my desk,
face up, with the Tao telling me, telling you.

Your blue ballpoint pen dents the paper yet
and I remember those big banjo hands
guiding chisels through wood, gripping a shovel
to kill a rattlesnake when you had no choice.

You told me you designed a course around
the books we read, lazy afternoons in the trailer –
Miller, Ginsberg, Kerouac and Burroughs,
their words filling our time between fucks.

And then they filled your students' time and yours
and mine again beyond the days of sex,
the living years, then dying time that even so
lets a yellow letter lie here still.

Hotel

From our room
five floors up, he swings
over the courtyard,
hinged by one hand
and one foot,
buff naked, out
into the night rain.

His red hair
is everywhere
proving its natural
truth at crevices
and folds, head hair
lank with rain, drips
on his shoulders.

He straightens
his arms, higher,
locks his knees,
swings out again,
perfect with Leonardic
proportions, rain
streaked, glistening.

In the circle,
he was anchored.
In the square,
there was no
assurance. Love,
I decided would
be like this,

only each time,
one floor up.
He was the real
thing, against
which I measured
breadth and depth
of love and rooms.

Dare

Let's talk about death, she said.
You first.

And he began with an oak tree, a glade
a blackbird and rain
then he nodded to her

and she began with ribbons on lapels
scissors and Hebrew prayers
then she nodded to him

and he went on with winter
leaves decaying, breath and emptiness
and he nodded to her

and she went on wanting to tear
her clothing to shreds
then she nodded to him

and he went on staring through branches
trying to count the few leaves left
then he nodded to her

and she went on with the fear of
unravelling threads, looser and looser
and she nodded to him

and he went on standing in the doorway
with the mourner's book in his hand
and he nodded to her

and she went on with her ripped blouse
hanging from her shoulders, shaking

and he went on with his bare hands open –
as she fell against him he held her up.

Let's talk about death
she said

and he closed his mouth and arms
and shoulders around her, refusing.

Fallowfield

He called my name, so I guess I knew him.
I knelt down on the pavement, looked straight

across into his eyes, his unkempt face,
smelled the alcohol, and yes, he looked familiar.

I touched the sleeve of his army coat lightly
as I spoke. He didn't resist my questions.

Yes, he'd been drinking, but just to kick
the ass of boredom. I can see that, I said.

But was he getting enough food? Enough sleep?
Were doorways really warm enough at night?

My eyes watered in the cold and a tear
swelled onto my cheek, then spilled.

His hand moved instinctively, like a lover's
to catch the tear on the curve of his index finger.

Nearly at its destination, he pulled back
the hand and dropped his eyes to the ground.

How could we have forgotten
what the two of us were doing here?

Married Man

He holds the name
of his wife like a hand grenade,
ready to lob at his lover's feet
whenever she goes too far.

'Susan and I,' he says,
'went shopping and Susan bought... '
His lover covers her ears,
and sticks out her tongue.

She is at risk,
he is at risk,

and certainly,
so is what's her name.

Late

That night, using his key,
entering on tiptoe, moving
closer and closer to the bed,
peering over them,

he couldn't imagine who
that strange man was.
Even so, he left
the rolled-up gift behind.

A Navajo rug
for his faithless lover,
the tree of life
cut down in front of him.

Oh, giver of gifts, long dead,
is it too late to say
she too didn't know who
that strange man was –

the one she'd wandered after
in the dark, afraid
she might lose you, her love,
her life, along the way.

His Book

She moves his book from table to desk to chair
to bed, hoping it will become part of her
just by picking it up, then letting it lie close.

She wants his sentences and photographs
to swim in her head, course through her blood,
then trickle into her dreams and conversation

painlessly, comfortably, enjoyably
as if reading were indeed a leisure activity,
for holidays while sunbathing on the beach.

She wants to read his new book more than any book.
She knows what he went through to write it,
what his subjects sacrificed to let him in.

Pages 40 and 41 are a double-spread photograph
and she stays with this image, relieved, relaxed,
her eyes free to roam without diminishing results.

She sees a room, stark with three red sofas,
almost tasteful cushions, white walls, and a man
with self-inflicted tattoos on his hands.

It's a place where no one lives, nothing is owned.
From reading a bit, she knows the man's name and why
he's alone in the great sadness of this refuge room.

This book isn't long. It's only 128 pages.
She flicks them, stopping and starting, back to front
letting the text pass and the red sofas ease her.

Marriage

'My wife left me,'
said the man who never loved his wife
and was glad she'd gone. He was
delighted that her face would never be
on the pillow beside him again,
that his parents-in-law would
no longer be related to him.

He liked the loose, untidy feel
of the house, the fridge, his drawers,
the garage and the lawn.
He had stopped being a keeper
of wife, house, appearances,
but he didn't like the sentence,
'My wife left me.'

Separation

This part, she said, is yours,
this part is mine.

But he reached across her,
lifted it all at once
without regard for subdivision.

Stop, she cried, but it was too late.
Already he was backing
through the door with arms full.

He just couldn't face
where he was going with it.

Old Jewish Men

One's in Camden, playing to a lucky few
one's in my iPhone, singing the darkness down
one's on my pull-down train-table explaining work
one's on the Stockport platform waiting to take me home –

these touch-stones, these heart keys,
these love looseners, these joy snares,
these home holders, these bread bringers
these grief-laden-history packhorses of
loss, of sorrow-swells and blind suffering –

they just tag along with me in recognition –
my senior railcard, my plug-in headphones,
my against the odds willingness to believe,
so I stick with them, they stick with me.

Yesterday

Was it the horizontal light, the warmth
or how low the sun was in the sky,
that so unsettled the ducks yesterday?

The river kept on going to Liverpool
all afternoon and the ducks
pulled upstream just to stay put.

I wished you could have seen
the reddening leaves, the bright berries
splattered against the Wedgwood sky,

glints of blue, green and silver,
then tail feathers suddenly upended
as the Mersey dragged itself through.

Autumn was begging a debt from summer
in a kind of devil's payoff. Something
sacred surely must have been lost

in the river's surly rush, and then found
again in that great relief of light.
This, all of it, is what you missed.

II

Kisses and Harps

Kisses

At Arm's Length

Not on the tip of her nose
to spite her face,
not on her stuck-out neck
or knowing for sure
like the back of her hand,
her inner eye, her sixth sense
her elbow from her knee,
a certain feeling in her bones
the arm and a leg of loss
a belly laugh of gain
her Adam's apple stuck,
a wishbone wedged.
She grabbed her own blue
breasts in the dark
trembling, afraid
of her own nipples.

Primary Colours

Injecting radioactive dye to find the sentinel lymph node

She had turned blue in parts
visible and invisible, internal and external
immediate and time lagged
to surprise her in the future.

Red would have been useless,
fading to pink around her nipples,
her blood becoming paler day by day,
her lips losing what redness there was.

Yellow fades on contact with the flesh
trailing traits of two-day bruises
more like shadows than like pigment,
tinges dying slowly without the sun.

It had to be blue, truest blue,
so she resigned herself to let her body
stain its every process in the hope
of outwitting it, getting there first.

How to Make Breasts Disappear

Be eleven in the summer
wearing boy's trunks.
Then swim carefree as a fish.
Are these breasts?

At twelve, try a training bra
to flatten these brash interlopers.
Nip them in the bud.
Are these breasts?

Cover them with your hands
to hide them from your lover.
Be coy as armour.
Are these breasts?

Harden, as if kapok filled,
leaking, throbbing, on day three
after your baby is born.
Are these breasts?

Lie on your back
with your hands behind your head.
Only gentle mounds remain.
Are these breasts?

There are other ways
to make breasts disappear,
but for these, you must give up
your body entirely.

Ticks and Kisses

Up to one in ten women over fifty
might be writing a confessional poem
about one of her breasts right now,

though some of these women
might choose to write about something else.
Prostate cancer for example, or husbands.

Others might never write a poem
about anything, leaving space for
some women to write about both breasts.

'Amputation' is not a good subject
for poetry. That's what most people think
who were surveyed at a seaside resort last week.

It had the smallest number of ticks beside it
though the survey manager was not surprised.
Enhancements always beat reductions.

Love got more. Substantially more.
Breasts got more still, inside bathing suits.
Fewer when they had escaped their cups.

The place on the chest where a breast
once was is not a topic which attracted
any ticks at all. Nor kisses, nor caresses.

Health Scare

She counted her dead lovers as carefully
as she would have had they been alive,
tipping each head back, opening each one's eyes
and staring straight through their pupils
directly into their wandering souls.

Don't worry about decay or effects of cremation!
She didn't use their actual bodies for this count.
Instead she called to mind the moment each one
had said he loved her, just before a kiss
and then soon after, falling asleep in her arms.

The live ones went uncounted simply due to
their own routines, assorted chores and joys
as free men to whom she owed nothing
and who expected nothing in return. The line
was clear between her lovers, dead and alive,

clearer than the lines she drew around herself,
uncertain where she stopped and started,
lived and died, where her vision reached
and where it fizzled out, cutting itself dead.
She reached instinctively to take her pulse.

Her phone rang, her email chimed and the post
was full of cards, but she kept right on fading
away from her own children's flowers,
blurring before their lovingly prepared food
and the fresh fruit in their hands.

Non-Poetics

I signed the agreement.
You may, I say,
burn my flesh
with radioactive rays.
Go ahead, feel free –
ionise my molecules.

I take off my lead vest,
covering a concrete
encrusted bodice and
lay these on the chair,
baring my chest,
non-metaphorically.

There is very little
poetry here in the
literal way of large wall
mounted machines –
their buzzing, their
automatic repositioning.

Fractionate my dose
so I can come often,
each day looking forward
to the accumulation
of debilitating effects.
The skin gets redder.

Moist desquamation
is not sexy like it sounds.
The skin has thinned
and begun to weep.
I admire its honesty,
restraint from simile.

Sleeping

Sleeping into the rock band
sleeping into the traffic
sleeping into the gentle afternoon
into the hornets' nest, the stars,
into the night scented stock.

Sleeping into the filing cabinet
sleeping into river floods
sleeping into the cows' hooves
and into their mouths
and into the mangled landscape.

Sleeping into the chestnut trees
and into the shaded lawn,
each year, with less and less light,
sleeping into the space
I tried so hard to keep clear

before I fell asleep.

Lost Souls from Christie Hospital

Souls are escaping onto Wilmslow Road
in ones and twos like wobbling bubbles
which have risen and punctured slowly.
Unceremoniously, they're released
through sliding glass curtains to the cold.

Once out, their confusion is apparent.
Left and right seem to be the same to them,
yet their heads keep turning from side to side
as if a preference would emerge on merit
and they'd know from their hearts where to go.

Do the souls want coffee in cramped cafés
tucked in beside the pubs of Withington?
Or would they prefer to find a newsagent,
buy a paper, sweets and just keep walking
in the direction of estate agents and banks?

They turn toward the cafés, arm in arm
and walk deliberately toward some promise
of fulfilment, sipping caffè lattes, sitting
at wood-grained plastic tables – souls,
half remembering their human bodies.

Radiotherapy

Her underwear provoked comment,
her punctuality was questioned,
her choice of body lotion vetoed.

Her cough was simply not allowed.
Her breathing was too deep,
her arm not quite high enough.

Her smock should have been on,
bra-less, by the time she was called.
The only signal was people in the room.

What was her name, her address?
Five new people every day, nameless.
Leave appointment card, name side up.

Mount the table, let them move her,
line up her back on a narrow green plank,
her head in a hard rubber cup.

Unsnap the poppers, the felt tip pen's
all set to make new balance marks.
The machine's pre-positioned, on target.

Five people leave the room.
The buzzing comes and goes,
lights go on and off. They're back.

'What are your plans for the weekend?'
said an unnamed man. She stared at him,
slid from the table, vanished.

Ray Charles visits Suite 1, Radiotherapy Department
Christie Hospital, Manchester, England

Looking at the ceiling day after day –
the Siemen's air-conditioning vent,
protruding speakers, lights,
the soundproof panels,
she tolerated the radio's
monotonousness until today
when, out of the blue,
Ray Charles dropped into the room
with 'What'd I Say?'
and she followed his every word,
each bluesy chord,
the entire pulse of him
wondering how and why
he'd found her in England
after all these years
since the time she'd heard him
in California playing
that big arena in 1965.
Wow! He was amazing then
and was, she thought, pretty wonderful
today too, recorded, invisible, even dead
and probably no longer blind
since he'd had vision till he was seven
and might be able to see again
if there were any kind of justice
or afterlife –
her boyfriend had held
her hand that night
as if he'd been afraid
she might leave him
the way husbands put their arms
around their wives
in the waiting room
hoping the wives won't die soon
and leave them and their children
alone the way she herself was alone

in the waiting room and now on the table,
till Ray came in –
she wished she'd had her red dress on.

Harps

Pronouncement

This is big, really big.
Now I can feel how big
it is, she says, examining
a scramble of red grey
hair snared in one hand.

Max

She tells her grandson everything,
except the trampoline,
will still go on.

I'll be just fine
she tells him on the phone,
reminding him how much

his other granny loves him,
suggesting ways to play with her,
games to make her fun.

It won't be long before I'm home,
she says to him. You'll see.
My treatment will be over soon.

How I love you, Max.
She replaces the receiver,
bends her knees, her ankles flex.

In love, she tests herself –
the faintest semblance of a jump.

Gift House

The house itself, a gift, and in the house are gifts –
the food, the telephone, the messages are gifts,
even pills are gifts from the State of California,
our stories are gifts, the way we whisper at night,
the cooking, the shopping and the cleaning by day
are gifts and the runs to the video store are gifts
and the DVDs are gifts of movies from the 50s.
The porch gives lumbering Adirondack chairs,
forever being repositioned as the sun moves round.
I take our kitchen waste outside to compost bins.
Children fill the path with bikes and baseball bats.
They chalk flowers on the sidewalk below our door,
yellow, exactly placed, these tulip heads point up
as we look down from the porch, think of going out.
Instead we picture ourselves with one another, smiling
on the steps as our stories give themselves away.

Care Givers

Of course,
we are interchangeable,
one of the women said,

(as the grey cat
landed on the porch,
from next door's roof

and padded softly
in between our feet
toward the railings' shade,

settling finally
with her white paws
out in front of her).

Candour

Did she hear everything? Yes,
measurements, in three dimensions,
the fact that it's inoperable,
the ropy path the mind might take.
Yes, everything was said to her.

Did they say what time was left?
No, no one spoke to her of time.
Time makes all the days too real,
and no one wants to count them –
numberless, glorious, blessed.

Dwight Way

'We're going to the beach –
not to make you jealous
or anything,' he says
packing his car with folding
chairs, coolers, bats, leading
with his sunburned nose,
kids bobbing up and down
around his knees, on a side
street, magnolias in bloom,
and we're laughing as we say
back, 'not jealous at all – enjoy!'
and he says (this perfect
stranger) 'I will, I will,'
as we turn right onto Grant
with our own stories –
the circus days of baths
in the kitchen, tightropes,
tractors, sugarbeet,
and the guest who gave birth
upstairs like a blessing
on the house, with ease.

Harp in the Sick Room

for Roberta

If a harp comes into the room
before anyone thinks of angels
plucking harp strings in heaven,
could the whole thing be forestalled?

The harpist just gets on with it –
letting the music come to her
out of thin air into her fingers
as the rest of us wonder about

chickens and eggs and cause
and effect and rushing in
like fools to grab paradise
by the balls for our beloved.

Dying

Dying wakes you up quietly, wafting
into your nostrils (or so I imagine)
simply by virtue of not renewing itself.
Lifelessness backs up in your room.

'I've got to get out of here!'
you say earnestly into the monitor
which has listened all night long
to your breath, not ever expecting
a whole rational sentence.

By the time I rush to your side
and raise the head of your bed
there isn't a whiff of dying left
and your sentence is simply to go on.

Asleep and Awake

She's asleep with the cat
and awake with the sea

and in between that
she's talking to me.

Not casual chat –
we've no gossip to share.

She takes off her hat
though her hair is spare.

Her words seem to scat
and meaning is rare

as she straddles the line,
her prayer in the glare

of the sun in decline,
and it sets as we swear

she's awake with the sea
and asleep with the cat,

but she'll whisper to me,
long, long after that.

Resting Place

I was driving and you were toiling
to get your words in some kind of order
for the enormous meaning they needed.
After was the only one that pointed
to the end and what would come next.
No signs were visible from the road.

That day we stopped along the coast
again and again looking for the place
you had chosen to be *after*.
It didn't feel morbid at all – more like
choosing a campsite on a cliff
or the best view of the sea.

Finally, in a lay-by I saw a metal sign
for Elk Community Cemetery.
It labelled high ground behind a fence
between the highway and the sea below.
We climbed through sagging wires
to check the view, and yes, it *was* the best.

Home Funeral

I find the best photos I have of you
and Google the number of miles between
here and there – 5,768, more or less.

I want to know what I'm up against.
No one answers their phones any more –
they're all at your house with you.

I don't know Hebrew prayers
or songs, the blessings or rituals
though I'm sure candles will be needed.

I take the necklace you chose for me
from your jewellery box, us in the mirror,
you holding the clasp from behind.

Without guidance or a template,
I scatter these objects of love
and keep the matches handy.

I like it this way.
It will be a reckless funeral –
something like the cliff edge you chose for yourself.

The Midst

In the midst of prayers
to purify your body,
while the water is poured
and dabbed away with love,
my call is left to ring
itself out through the house,
then onto the answering machine.

A click and your voice is saying
'Hello, this is Ella. I'm home.'

The Twenty-four Hours

I know they are washing you now,
carefully in that room of yours
– those limbs of yours, each one,
and goodness knows, that trunk!

They'll be sweeping aside what's left
of your flaming hair from your brow.
They'll be meticulous, vigilant,
prayers slipping from their lips,
songs replacing heaviness.

Tonight they'll bring sleeping bags
like canoes around the mother ship
and berth beside you until dawn.
Even so, I think you'll sail to me.

In Jewish custom, the person who died must be buried within twenty-four hours.
During this time the body is bathed and never left alone.

III
Our Lives

Taffeta

We heard her rustling down the stairs,
drummer's brushes on a hi-hat cymbal
and then on the lino the click and tap,
of high heeled patent leather
and the softer sound of dancing soles.
She spun around like Cyd Charisse.
Kids, how do I look?

Her favourite dress, black and white taffeta
with its New Look skirt needed crinolines
to flounce the bottom out.
Her charm bracelet jingled and Chanel No. 5
vied with our burgers and French fries.

Then she did her *I'm ravishing* look,
pursed her lips, hand on her hip.
Skip and I started to laugh, she laughed
and Spotty yelped and wriggled.

Then it was time for good night kisses,
the *I love you but I'm going out dancing* kisses
accounting for lipstick, hair, stocking seams.
We'd practised other Saturday nights,
holding our arms out straight in the air –
two little promises not to rumple or smudge.

We knew that children were not the only things
on earth that counted.

The jitterbug did,
and the rumba.

Name

The name was said just once
in the United States of America
and then forgotten for generations.
My daughter had to coax it loose from cousins
who weren't sure, but nearly sure.
They knew the year, the crossing, the language,
but the name – Kugen, Krugen, Kruger?

Ellis Island clerks were slipshod with names
Jewish? Give him Cohen.
As for me, I didn't need
to know my grandpa's name,
playing with him on the floor in a pool of sun
filtered through grimy windows
Sundays, in a Newark apartment block.

Contract for Love and Death

Fine print? There was none.
We simply said the usual 'I do's'
and let our lives spin out
to love and die in equal lots.

My mother had become a Long Island
Fuchsia, as crimson and as purple
as pixie boots with turned up toes,
but her bark then dried to paper.

Your father, by the Danube, sprouted leaves
of birch, as tender as his chalky sheath,
as light as twenty languages becoming one.
He spoke to us for Europe – all of it.

My brother was a messenger of choice.
'Choose everything,' he said. And did.
Too soon he was an air-born echo
of activity, overspent, still whispering.

Your mother was a sporty Sunbeam
in the tropics – a convertible, bright red.
Every time she stopped, she started up
again, twice as fast – until the last.

Her husband was a map of Africa,
unstable as Uranium 235, imprisoned
with Gershwin's *Rhapsody in Blue*,
and then set free by Bach.

My father danced his way
down Broadway, empty headed,
passing silver dollars through his heart –
dropping boutonnières like crumbs.

Your brother spun his wheels so fast
that his Ferrari heart was flung against
the dashboard of the Ivory Coast and landed
in the ocean beyond Abidjan.

Look at us, still wheeling on our
tread-stripped hearts through all this life,
parked next to one another as we agreed,
near the exit from these multi-storeys.

Jazzer

My brother can dance
to jazz and rock and roll
though he trained through
foxtrot, rumba and waltz
which is not true of every
dead man you can think of.
Mostly the others lie around
or visit old friends on earth
without evoking anything.
No sneaking up in the dark —
they just appear in a hazy
outline at the end of
long carpeted corridors.
My brother (like our Pop)
drops in on a drum roll
and a cymbal crash,
a trumpet blast, tenor sax —
he's just so fucking
finger-snapping cool.
Nothing creepy about him.
He brings his friends
along on vinyl — The MJQ,
Miles, Brubeck and Coltrane.
Every time I think of him
he's at a Newport party
and never forgets to put me
on the guest list.

Winter on Long Island

When it snowed all day, we'd find you in our living room
after school, Scotch on the rocks with our mother.

When the snow-felted roads of Long Island were ice,
you'd stay and go to school next day from our house.

When you trained the wrestlers to arch into neck rolls,
you'd strut back and forth reciting Vachel Lindsay.

When you taught *A Child's Christmas in Wales*
our class divided the voices, then spoke as one.

When the *dumb numb thunder-storm of white torn
Christmas cards* settled on the postman, I'd cry each time.

When your wife died, every high school girl you'd loved
became more beautiful and I, the most beautiful of all.

When my brother died, you lifted the night sky
with rumblings of verse, blue-knuckled and shattering.

Then the headlong moon bundled me down the street
till all I could hear was the ringing of bells inside me.

Italics from Dylan Thomas, A Child's Christmas in Wales

Till Graduation

Do I have to drag you down the Miracle Mile
again to window-shop or into the Ham and Eggery
for a Coke? Or will it be the Medical Centre
where Annie's mother died a little every day,
rose by rose from the florist.

Annie must have known what was coming,
fluffing the pillows and changing the water
in the glass with the bent straw, knowing it mattered.
The rosebuds in the tiny vase were essential.
Combing her mother's hair was a ritual.

News of cheerleading try-outs was crucial.
But to me, this was just the routine stop we made
every day on the way home from school
like other things we would do till graduation.
But we didn't do this for very long.

We were too young for funerals. All of us went
and the boys were silly at the house afterwards.
The girls held trays of food and glowered
at the boys who simply couldn't toe the line
and somehow got away with it.

Someone passed a love note behind
the satin sofa and it dropped.
Annie, small waisted, red lipped, was beautiful.
Her father looked like a movie star
and her sister wore white gloves.

Each of us tried to follow the list
of things we would do till graduation.
We who still had our mothers,
had our mothers' blessings that day,
one of the first days to split us apart.

Deceased, Class of 1959

He, last seen getting out of a 1955 Chevrolet
in the parking lot by the entrance to the gym,
chewing gum, basketball boots with tied laces
over his shoulder, no hurry, time to spare.

She was jumping with the other cheerleaders,
arms stretched, heels kicked up, back arched,
shouting 'Manhasset, Manhasset, yeah!'
as if being just like the others would do the trick.

That's when they saw each other last, just glancing
the way boys do that 'corner of the eye thing'
and girls shoot quick looks they never own up to
because, after all, they'd see each other tomorrow.

Giveaway

They planned their giveaway
to be a hailstorm, scattering
beyond the Strangeways tower.

They tossed away everything
they could get along without,
dumped the lot like a yard sale

strewn across their uncut grass,
a heap of secrets and scams
about to get away.

On the sale day, she wondered
if compromised goods were
as good as they looked

and if they'd fetch enough,
to let them get rid of rackets
and rouses and jams,

but no. He hadn't priced up
anything, no tit-for-tat tags.
This giveaway was just that.

August

The eucryphia has started to blurt,
the magnolia grenade erupts as well,
both trees flowering so haphazardly
they prove August is much too late for peace.
An arsenal of blossoms bursts, engorged
on a sunny branch of the eucryphia,
just as an exploding magnolia bloom,
bigger than my two hands, bloats out of reach.
At home in August, it's a battleground.
Overcome by sweet fumes, I'm hacking back,
and tossing water wildly to rescue
parched azaleas and these limp hydrangeas.
I'm reduced to ambulance, fire truck.

We know it's not the same river every day

US Airways Flight 1549

No one named the species of birds
but they were described as oversized and brown,
perhaps to avoid villainising migrant populations
or their countries of origin.
But everyone knows they were Canada Geese
and we must promise not to love them less.
The river also played a role –
hero in waiting, waterway wide enough
to fit cargo ships, the plane and the rescue boats,
just south of the George Washington Bridge,
as the river flows out to the Verrazano Straits.

We know it's not the same river every day –
a new one keeps rising in the Tear of Clouds
high in the Adirondacks and makes its way
to Troy where the Mohawk River contributes,
and flows, under the great bridges to the city;

the Dunn Memorial span at Albany

the Rip Van Winkle Bridge in the Catskills

the Kingston-Rhinecliff with its under-deck truss

the Franklin D. Roosevelt Midway Bridge

the Walkway made from the fire damaged
Poughkeepsie Railroad Bridge

then under The Newburgh Beacon

the Bear Mountain Bridge in Peekskill

the Tappan Zee, crossing the widest point
from Nyack in Rockland to Tarrytown, Westchester

and nesting in every bridge along the way
are peregrine falcons, the fastest birds on earth

and finally under the George Washington Bridge
joining Upper Manhattan with Fort Lee New Jersey

a span more than a thousand metres wide

the place the pilot chose,
barely missing the bridge,
the pilot who knew how to glide as well as fly,
the pilot who calmly said to air traffic control
when offered a runway at La Guardia
or another across the river in New Jersey –
this pilot who knew to keep the nose of the plane down
and the speed of the plane up during descent,
and for the landing to bring the nose up
and let the plane fall – the pilot who said,
'We can't, were going to be in the Hudson.'

6 August, 1945

a survivor speaks

I was six
born in 1939
Six – old enough to remember

and the radio reminds me
every day this week –
there's only one week left

> *what do you remember?*
> *where did it happen? Draw your story*
> *then place it on this grid of Hiroshima*

my story after sixty years
what I saw what I did
I've never even told the dead

today I buy crayons
and felt tipped pens
and several sheets of thick paper

> *send a drawing with some words*
> *what you saw – who – where –*
> *name the street and the district*

god help me as I begin to draw –
is this the first time in my life?
I must have stopped drawing at six

a woman crouches
over a baby in our street
near one of the brand new fire troughs

I draw her hair – her clothes
her skin although I know all of these
have been scorched away already

and I draw the baby boy
beneath her although
I know he is already dead

I know the baby's name
but do not write it anywhere
I draw his hair although it's gone

I do not draw myself at six
my running legs running for my life
away from my mother my brother

Sometimes Snow

Sometimes snow lights up all the drowsy fields
at night like cool electric blankets spread
beneath the moon, reflecting what the moon
reflects without a thank you to the sun,
no nod of gratitude, since light is light,
night is night, allowing you to see the dark
and through it to the light of snow, how dark
dying into day, trying to keep light
before a fading thaw reminds the sun
it's indebted to an impartial moon
for offering a surface so blank, spread
out so thin, so willing across those fields.

Last night you went to Shropshire on the train
and saw everything. Darling, don't explain.

Prospect Cottage

Crouching in the shadow of Dungeness
is what they say about your cottage.

Living with Aids
is what they say about you.

Clinging to radioactive shingle
is what they say about your garden.

They say these things as they stroll
along the beach, kicking the tide line,

careless as cocks without condoms.
'Copulate here at your own risk'

is *not* what the words say on the side
of Prospect Cottage. They say 'the king rides'.

Mittens

From where I parked my car, green mittens on new snow
must have been visible from the only house across the road.
Inside, a family sat down to eat. I could see them.

Was it the moon, or just because the dog began to bark?
Was it because the snow had finally finished falling,
or because the mother watched the dog who watched the road?

In someone's eye a bit of green lodged like tangled wool,
eventually needing her attention. 'The Aga will be on all night,'
she may have thought as she pulled on her boots and gloves.

This is what I know: I lost my mittens. I found my mittens,
dry inside a plastic bag hanging from the aerial of my car.
It wasn't snowing any more. It was simply crisp and even.

Banana Crossing

Only because her carrier bag was clear
could anyone say for certain –
after all, who among us is an expert
in the ways of primates at traffic lights?

But there were witnesses –
six, seven, eight… even more.

She and the bag of bananas began
on the west side of the crossing
and headed east, guarded by green men
and no cars were allowed to turn.

She was not by herself, oh no –
her daughter pulled her along by force.

Not a pretty sight – a woman in her eighties
dragged along by a younger woman's tug.
If anyone thinks life happens day by day,
think again. It happens every second.

On the Way to the Wedding

A vat of cannelloni sauce simmered
as he yanked one tray of brownies at a time
and laid them criss-crossing each other in a stack.

He tugged one cheese after the next and held it
high turning it round on the axis of his arm to show
its particular shape, each one handsome, distinct.

Then wine, bread, olives and pickles were stacked
on the counter and packed into boxes
way too wide and too heavy for her to carry.

The burden of weddings and families and food
had no meaning for her today. She was simply
stopping at her son's deli on the way to the wedding.

Secret

You, almost fifty, bumming secret cigarettes
and then shoving mints in your mouth
as if you wouldn't get caught.

I see the boy in you.
I want him to kiss the back of my neck,
then turn around and run like hell.

The Crawl

He was heading toward an orange,
sure enough, when the right knee
inched forward, then inexplicably back
and the left hand reached out.

The left leg listed a little, tucking
itself under the opposite thigh
creating a quarter turn
bringing him up to sitting.

Each in turn had worked – left knee,
right hand lifting, padding down,
but then he lost his sights
in this sudden upright twist.

Grandma mobilised slowly.
She herself, a one-time champion
of the cross-pattern crawl, crawled
straight to him, starting from sitting.

The Only Mother

How could it be that my mother,
dead more than thirty years,
sits on this London train today?

'It's time,' she says, 'to pass it on,'
then turns her face to the window.
The window, I wonder, instead of me?

This line of mothers and daughters
tracks our speed, keeps to the rails,
as I head to my own dear girl

who sits by a window in a room
full of incubators and uncertainty.
She turns to her newborn daughter.

What can I give her today?
If I were the only mother
I would be sure to fail.

Better

Finally
like the sky lightening
behind the trees,
the trees lightening
behind the house,
before the sun
cracks the whole day
onto a plate,
yoke stunning itself
in a rich clear mass
of promises,
but I don't wake you
at 4 a.m. to say this.